HUNTERS

Written by Andrew Cleave
Illustrated by Stuart Lafford, Alan Male,
and Denys Ovenden

RSVP®
RAINTREE
STECK-VAUGHN
PUBLISHERS
The Steck-Vaughn Company

Austin, Texas

Editor: Kim Merlino
Project Manager: Julie Klaus

Library of Congress Cataloging-in-Publication Data
Cleave, Andrew
     Hunters / written by Andrew Cleave; illustrated by Stuart Lafford,
Alan Male, and Denys Ovenden.
        p.   cm. — (Pointers)
     Includes index.
     ISBN 0-8114-6191-2
     1. Predatory animals — Juvenile literature.   2. Predation (Biology) —
Juvenile literature. [1. Predatory animals.] I. Lafford, Stuart, ill.
II. Male, Alan, ill. III. Ovenden, Denys, ill. IV. Title. V. Series.
QL758.C58 1995
591.5'3—dc20   94-6005
                                            CIP
                                              AC

Printed and bound in the United States

1 2 3 4 5 6 7 8 9 0 VH 99 98 97 96 95 94

Foreword

Many animals have adapted to hunting other animals for their food. Hunters have sharp senses and quick reflexes. Most of them have one or two senses that are better developed than the others and that they use the most. For example, owls have excellent hearing but a poor sense of smell. Chameleons have very good eyesight but cannot hear well. Good eyesight, a strong sense of smell, acute hearing, and the ability to detect movements made by other animals all help hunters to find their food.

Many hunters can move quickly. The leopard seal, for example, is a very fast swimmer. Some hunters, however, move only slowly or lie in wait for their prey. Chameleons hide in their surroundings, becoming almost invisible. Many spiders spin webs of silk, waiting until the sticky threads trap an insect.

All hunters have special features that enable them to kill other animals. Many spiders use their sharp fangs and strong poison. Tigers have powerful, muscular bodies. Birds of prey have sharp claws and hooked beaks. This book describes some ways in which hunters find, catch, and kill their prey.

Contents

Spiders

Spiders are skilled at catching their prey, which is mostly insects. Nearly all spiders are venomous, and they can all spin silk.

Depending on the species, spiders use one of two methods to hunt. Some spiders, like the tarantula, move around looking for their prey. Other spiders build traps from the silk that they spin and lie in wait. The black widow, for example, spins a web. The threads of the webs are sticky and trap insects that fly or walk into them. Many spiders wrap their prey in silk until they are ready to eat it.

Trap-door spider

2 The trap-door spider lives in a burrow lined with silk and hidden by a silk-woven door. When an insect passes, the spider pushes the door open and pulls the prey into the burrow.

1 The tarantula can have a body length of almost 3 inches (7 cm). It has good eyesight for spotting its prey, powerful jaws to grasp and crush it, and a strong venom to kill it.

▲
Spiders have a set of fierce-looking jaws with two fangs, which pierce the skin of the prey and inject deadly venom. Spiders cannot chew their food, and so the jaws crush their prey.

Tarantula

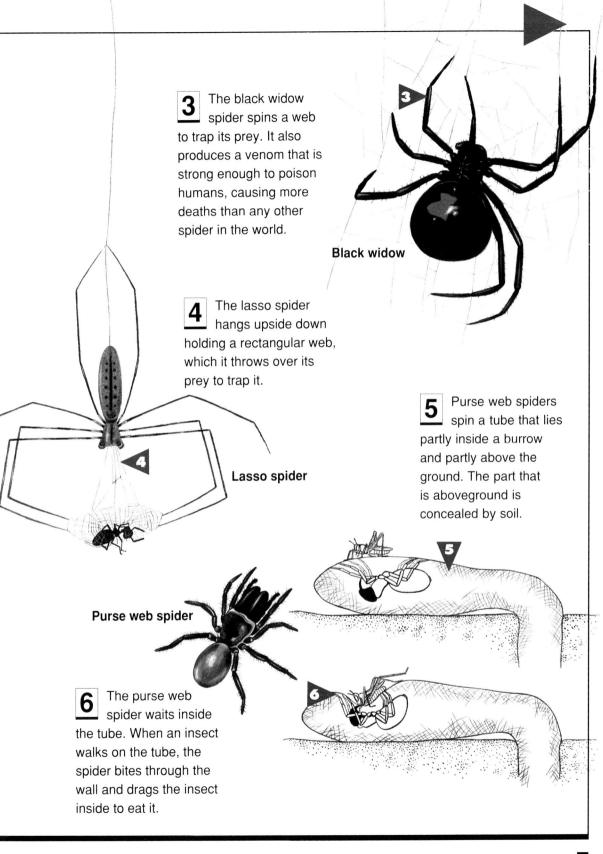

3 The black widow spider spins a web to trap its prey. It also produces a venom that is strong enough to poison humans, causing more deaths than any other spider in the world.

Black widow

4 The lasso spider hangs upside down holding a rectangular web, which it throws over its prey to trap it.

Lasso spider

5 Purse web spiders spin a tube that lies partly inside a burrow and partly above the ground. The part that is aboveground is concealed by soil.

Purse web spider

6 The purse web spider waits inside the tube. When an insect walks on the tube, the spider bites through the wall and drags the insect inside to eat it.

7

Insects

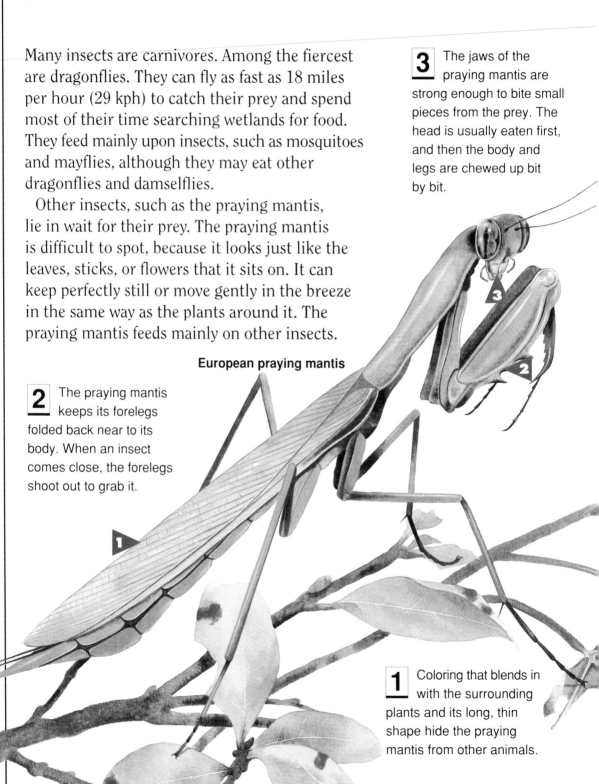

Many insects are carnivores. Among the fiercest are dragonflies. They can fly as fast as 18 miles per hour (29 kph) to catch their prey and spend most of their time searching wetlands for food. They feed mainly upon insects, such as mosquitoes and mayflies, although they may eat other dragonflies and damselflies.

Other insects, such as the praying mantis, lie in wait for their prey. The praying mantis is difficult to spot, because it looks just like the leaves, sticks, or flowers that it sits on. It can keep perfectly still or move gently in the breeze in the same way as the plants around it. The praying mantis feeds mainly on other insects.

3 The jaws of the praying mantis are strong enough to bite small pieces from the prey. The head is usually eaten first, and then the body and legs are chewed up bit by bit.

European praying mantis

2 The praying mantis keeps its forelegs folded back near to its body. When an insect comes close, the forelegs shoot out to grab it.

1 Coloring that blends in with the surrounding plants and its long, thin shape hide the praying mantis from other animals.

8

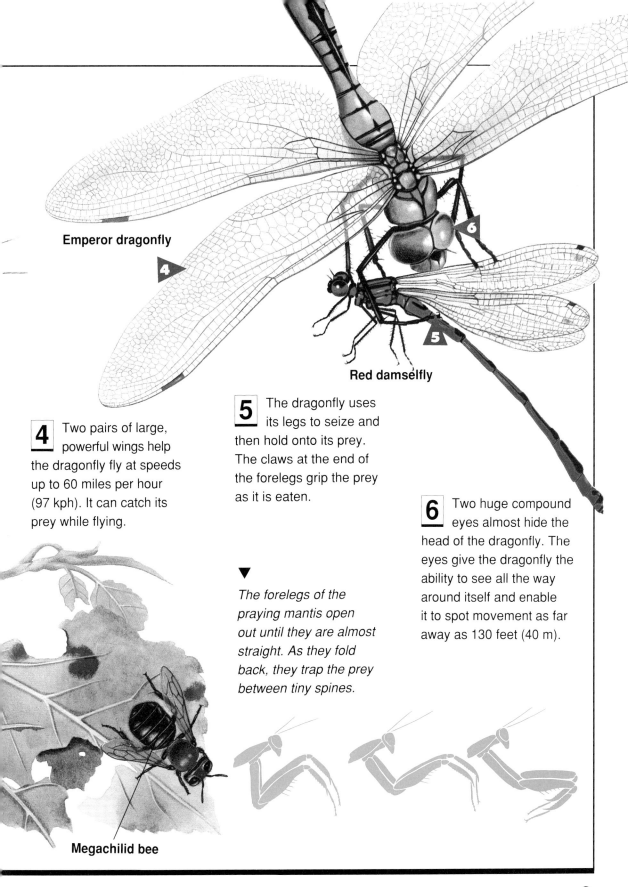

Emperor dragonfly

4

Red damselfly

5

6

4 Two pairs of large, powerful wings help the dragonfly fly at speeds up to 60 miles per hour (97 kph). It can catch its prey while flying.

5 The dragonfly uses its legs to seize and then hold onto its prey. The claws at the end of the forelegs grip the prey as it is eaten.

6 Two huge compound eyes almost hide the head of the dragonfly. The eyes give the dragonfly the ability to see all the way around itself and enable it to spot movement as far away as 130 feet (40 m).

▼

The forelegs of the praying mantis open out until they are almost straight. As they fold back, they trap the prey between tiny spines.

Megachilid bee

Mollusks

Mollusks are soft-bodied animals. Most types of mollusks live in shells. Many are herbivores (plant-eaters), but some are fierce predators that hunt other animals. The cone shell is found mainly in the Indo-Pacific Oceans. It looks like a harmless herbivore, but its shell conceals a sting that can paralyze and kill. Some cone shells hunt other mollusks, others hunt worms or fish. They lie in wait for their prey until it is close enough to attack.

The octopus is a mollusk that does not have a shell. It is found almost worldwide and is skilled at hiding away and then ambushing its prey, which is mainly fish and shellfish.

3 The octopus has excellent eyesight and can easily spot other animals. Keeping very still, its eyes follow every movement of its prey until the octopus can grab it.

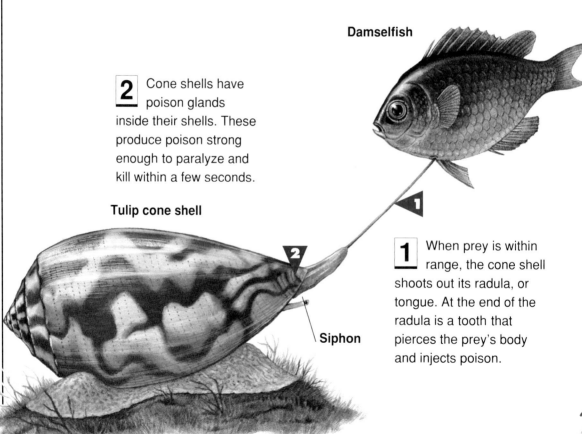

Damselfish

2 Cone shells have poison glands inside their shells. These produce poison strong enough to paralyze and kill within a few seconds.

Tulip cone shell

Siphon

1 When prey is within range, the cone shell shoots out its radula, or tongue. At the end of the radula is a tooth that pierces the prey's body and injects poison.

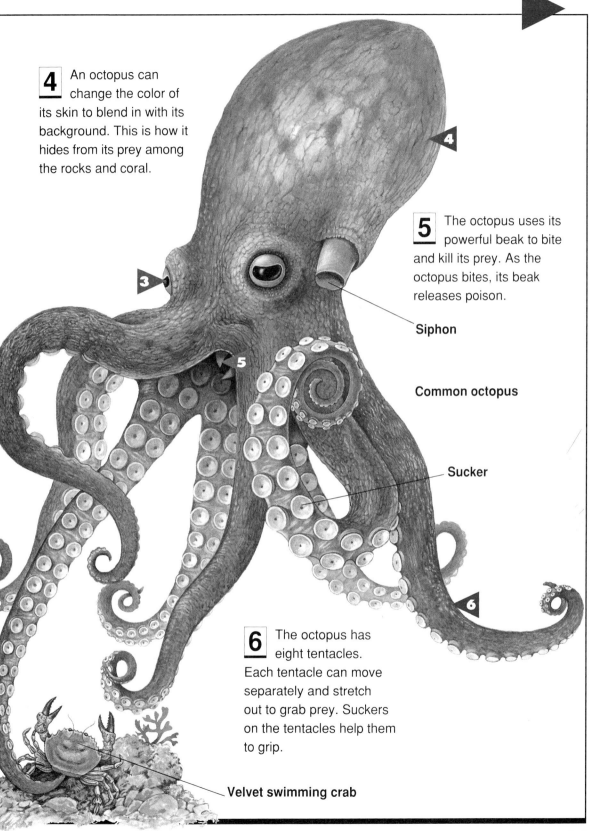

4 An octopus can change the color of its skin to blend in with its background. This is how it hides from its prey among the rocks and coral.

5 The octopus uses its powerful beak to bite and kill its prey. As the octopus bites, its beak releases poison.

Siphon

Common octopus

Sucker

6 The octopus has eight tentacles. Each tentacle can move separately and stretch out to grab prey. Suckers on the tentacles help them to grip.

Velvet swimming crab

Great White Sharks

The great white shark is usually found in warm waters and is one of the most feared predators of the sea. It mainly hunts sea lions, seals, otters, and fish, and has many different features that give it the strength and speed to catch its prey. The shark's most powerful weapon is its razor-sharp teeth. Its bite is 300 times more powerful than the bite of a human, allowing it to take huge chunks out of its prey. Many strange objects have been found inside the stomachs of great white sharks, including parts of automobiles and even torpedoes.

3 The skin of the shark is covered with tiny teethlike scales called placoid scales. They help to protect the shark and enable it to swim faster by reducing drag.

2 The shark has a streamlined, torpedo-shaped body. This helps it swim quickly and powerfully through the water.

1 Pilot fish swim alongside the shark. After the shark has eaten, the pilot fish clean up any scraps of food that are left behind.

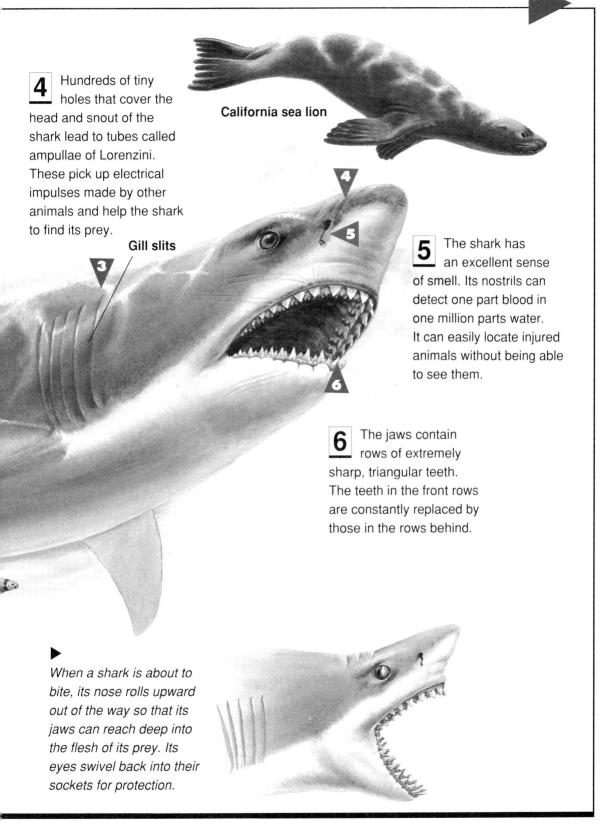

4 Hundreds of tiny holes that cover the head and snout of the shark lead to tubes called ampullae of Lorenzini. These pick up electrical impulses made by other animals and help the shark to find its prey.

California sea lion

Gill slits

5 The shark has an excellent sense of smell. Its nostrils can detect one part blood in one million parts water. It can easily locate injured animals without being able to see them.

6 The jaws contain rows of extremely sharp, triangular teeth. The teeth in the front rows are constantly replaced by those in the rows behind.

▶ *When a shark is about to bite, its nose rolls upward out of the way so that its jaws can reach deep into the flesh of its prey. Its eyes swivel back into their sockets for protection.*

Mongooses

2 Mongooses have between 34 and 40 teeth. The pointed front teeth clamp onto the head and jaws of the snake, eventually killing it. The back teeth tear flesh.

3 The mongoose has a very good sense of smell. This helps it to find animals in places where they are difficult to see, such as in tall grass.

1 When the mongoose attacks, the cobra rears up and spreads out the skin flaps beneath its head to look fierce. The cobra's quick reflexes enable it to make rapid strikes with its fangs.

Spectacled cobra

4 The mongoose's fur stands on end when it is fighting. This makes it look bigger than it really is, and the snake often only strikes at its fur and not at its skin.

The mongoose is a carnivorous (meat-eating) mammal. Although it is small, it is extremely fast and agile, and is able to attack large and dangerous animals, such as poisonous cobras. It also hunts much smaller animals, such as lizards, beetles, spiders, and scorpions. Most species of mongooses live in warm, dry places, especially in Africa and India. They usually hunt at night, although some species hunt during the day. In some countries, the mongoose is kept as a pet to keep homes and gardens free from rats, mice, and snakes.

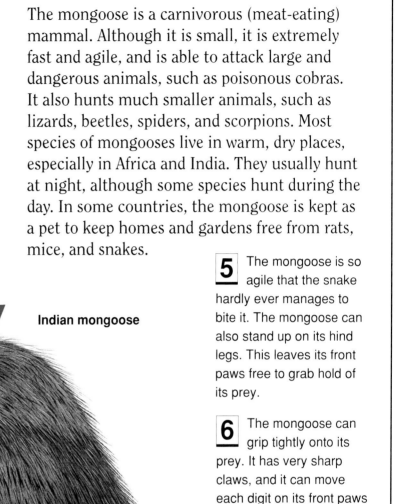

Indian mongoose

5 The mongoose is so agile that the snake hardly ever manages to bite it. The mongoose can also stand up on its hind legs. This leaves its front paws free to grab hold of its prey.

6 The mongoose can grip tightly onto its prey. It has very sharp claws, and it can move each digit on its front paws separately, similar to the way we can move our fingers.

Chameleons

Chameleons are slow-moving reptiles that are most frequently found in trees and bushes in the warmer parts of Europe, Africa, and Madagascar. They are usually between 6 and 10 inches (15 and 25 cm) long, although some can be as long as 24 inches (60 cm). Most species feed on insects, although some catch lizards and even birds and small mammals.

Chameleons are perfectly adapted to hunting from trees. Their feet and tails are so suited to gripping branches that they find it difficult to move on the ground. When their prey comes close enough, chameleons use their long, sticky tongues to catch it.

2 The skin of the chameleon changes color and pattern to blend in with its surroundings. This makes it difficult for the prey to see the chameleon.

1 By wrapping its tail around the branch, the chameleon is able to keep completely still as it waits for its prey to come close enough to catch.

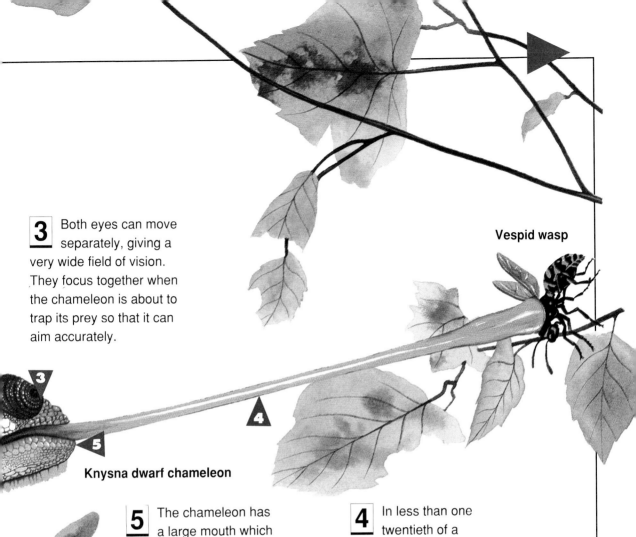

3 Both eyes can move separately, giving a very wide field of vision. They focus together when the chameleon is about to trap its prey so that it can aim accurately.

Vespid wasp

Knysna dwarf chameleon

5 The chameleon has a large mouth which is ideal for swallowing its prey in one gulp. Its long tongue folds easily inside the mouth when it is not being used.

4 In less than one twentieth of a second, the sticky tongue shoots out of the mouth and catches an insect. The tongue draws back into the mouth, pulling the insect with it.

6 Rough skin on the chameleon's feet and five strong claws enable it to grip and climb without slipping. They help to anchor the chameleon firmly when its tongue shoots out.

Boa Constrictors

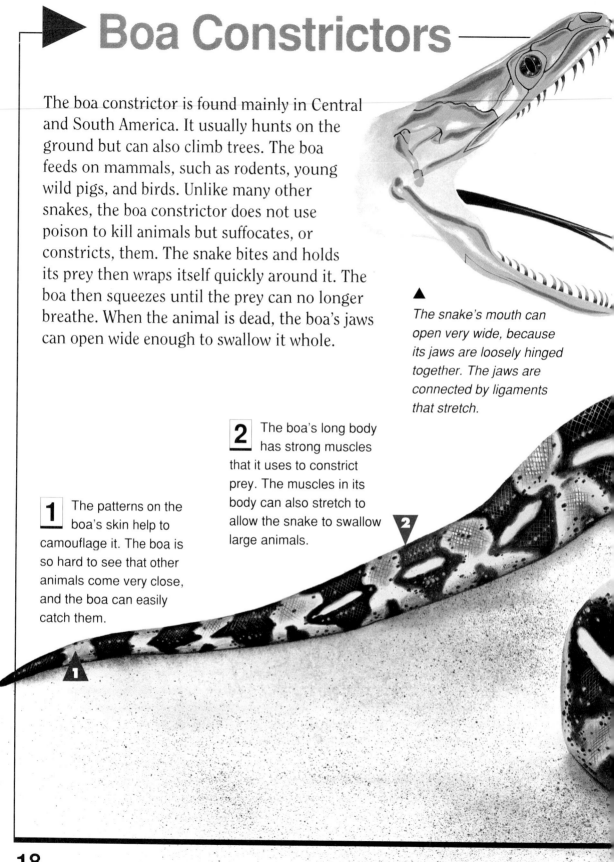

The boa constrictor is found mainly in Central and South America. It usually hunts on the ground but can also climb trees. The boa feeds on mammals, such as rodents, young wild pigs, and birds. Unlike many other snakes, the boa constrictor does not use poison to kill animals but suffocates, or constricts, them. The snake bites and holds its prey then wraps itself quickly around it. The boa then squeezes until the prey can no longer breathe. When the animal is dead, the boa's jaws can open wide enough to swallow it whole.

▲
The snake's mouth can open very wide, because its jaws are loosely hinged together. The jaws are connected by ligaments that stretch.

2 The boa's long body has strong muscles that it uses to constrict prey. The muscles in its body can also stretch to allow the snake to swallow large animals.

1 The patterns on the boa's skin help to camouflage it. The boa is so hard to see that other animals come very close, and the boa can easily catch them.

3 The forked tongue flicks in and out of the boa's mouth to pick up chemicals in the air. The boa analyzes the chemicals and identifies those that are of its prey.

4 The boa's mouth can open wide enough to swallow prey larger than its head. Its teeth point backward, allowing the boa to swallow its prey easily.

5 A row of pits along the snake's upper lips sense any variation in the temperature nearby. In this way, the boa can detect the body heat of another animal.

6 The boa tightens its squeeze each time its prey breathes in. Once it can no longer breathe, the boa swallows it headfirst.

Rat

Eagle Owls

Eagle owls live in dark forests in Europe and North Africa. Their body length is 28 inches (71 cm), and they are powerful hunters, mainly searching for their prey at night. They rely most of all upon their hearing to detect their prey and can hear the quietest of rustling sounds made by small animals. They are able to glide silently and quickly through the forests, catching a variety of animals, including those that run very fast. Eagle owls hunt small mammals, such as voles and rabbits, and sometimes larger mammals, such as roe deer fawns. They also hunt birds, reptiles, and even insects. They swoop down with their talons outstretched, ready to seize their prey.

▲
The wing feathers are fringed along the edge so that air flows easily over them, cutting down on sound when the owl flies.

Ear tuft

European eagle owl

5

3

2

6

2 Eagle owls have hooked beaks, which they use for tearing large animals to pieces before eating them. They usually swallow small animals whole.

Rabbit

1

1 The feathered talons of the eagle owl are strong enough to kill an animal by piercing the flesh and to grip the animal as the owl flies away.

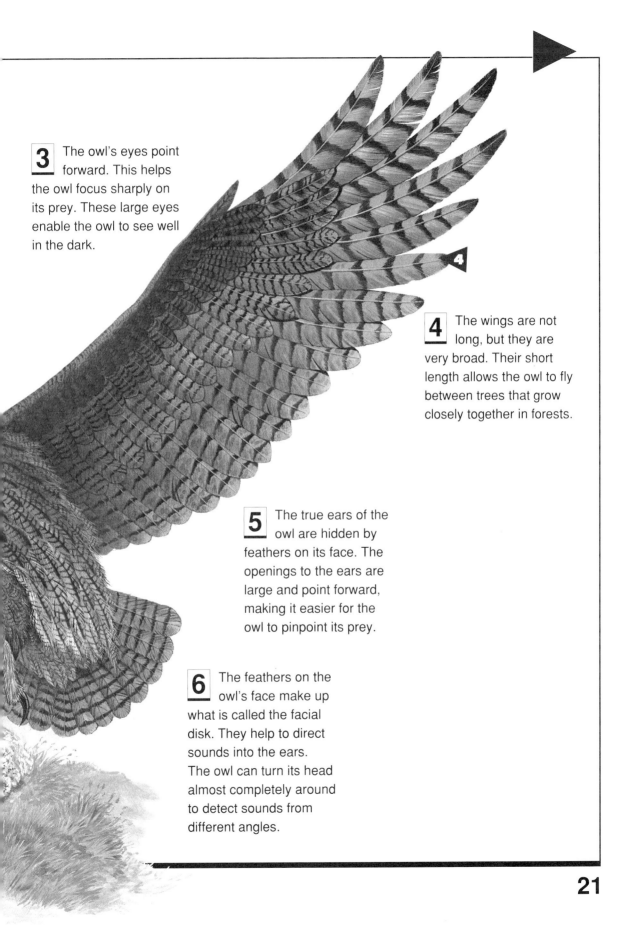

3 The owl's eyes point forward. This helps the owl focus sharply on its prey. These large eyes enable the owl to see well in the dark.

4 The wings are not long, but they are very broad. Their short length allows the owl to fly between trees that grow closely together in forests.

5 The true ears of the owl are hidden by feathers on its face. The openings to the ears are large and point forward, making it easier for the owl to pinpoint its prey.

6 The feathers on the owl's face make up what is called the facial disk. They help to direct sounds into the ears. The owl can turn its head almost completely around to detect sounds from different angles.

Secretary Birds

3 Secretary birds have very broad, strong wings. Sometimes they use their wings to beat their prey, especially snakes.

▲ When the secretary bird flies, it shows the full size of its wings. They have a span of over 6 feet (2 m), and their black and gray pattern is unlike that of any other bird of prey.

Secretary birds live in the grasslands of Africa. They have long legs and a body over 3 feet (1 m) long. They are different from many other birds in the way they hunt. Secretary birds do not fly to find their prey but look for it on the ground. Secretary birds are very skilled at catching snakes, but they also eat lizards, insects such as locusts, small mammals, and even other birds. They hunt in pairs or in small groups that keep in contact with one another by hooting.

Secretary birds take their name from the feathers on top of their heads. These look just like the quill pens that secretaries wrote with a long time ago.

2 Secretary birds have very long legs, making it easy to run through grass and chase prey. Scales of hard skin protect the legs from snakebites.

1 A secretary bird's feet are very strong. It uses its feet to kill prey. The bird stamps on its prey's head, or it may perhaps kick out, stunning it with one blow.

4 Secretary birds have very good eyesight. Their sight is three times sharper than ours, and they can spot the tiniest movement of animals far away.

5 The skin around the base of the beak and eyes is bare. This means that the secretary bird can feed without food sticking to any of its feathers.

6 The secretary bird's beak is hooked, enabling it to tear flesh from its prey. Sometimes it holds its prey in its beak, banging it against the ground to kill it.

Spitting cobra

Fish-eating Bats

Fish-eating bats, also known as fishing bulldog bats, live along sheltered rivers and lakes in South America. They hunt mainly for fish, but sometimes for insects. They have short, orange-yellow fur which is well adapted for shedding water, and so they do not become waterlogged when they fish for their prey. Flying slowly, close to the water, the bats locate fish by detecting ripples made by their prey. Once ripples are detected, they swoop down, snatching a fish up with their claws and lifting it from the water. Fish-eating bats swallow small fish as soon as they have caught them. They carry larger fish away to a perch to eat them.

3 The bat's ears are very large. They can easily pick up echoes of sounds the bat produces.

2 The bat produces high-pitched sounds, which the nostrils direct to the water. The sounds bounce against the ripples of any fish at the water's surface.

▲ *Sounds emitted from the bat's nostrils bounce off objects and return to its ears as echoes. This system, called echolocation, enables the bat to locate its prey.*

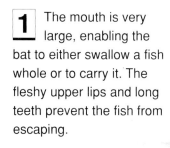

1 The mouth is very large, enabling the bat to either swallow a fish whole or to carry it. The fleshy upper lips and long teeth prevent the fish from escaping.

4 Large, broad wings enable the bat to fly rapidly over water and catch a fish as it appears at the surface. Sometimes the bat needs to swim and uses its wings as oars.

5 The long legs of the fish-eating bat help it to reach the fish. The legs are very strong and can easily support the weight of the fish.

6 The sharp claws can quickly pierce the slippery skin of a fish. The toes are flat so that they can easily slide through the water as the bat reaches for the fish.

Pike cichlid

Leopard Seals

The leopard seal is the largest seal in the Antarctic waters and the only one that regularly feeds on both birds and mammals. Its huge mouth and strong teeth, and its habit of attacking other large seals, make it a much feared predator. It usually lives on the edge of an ice shelf, where it can easily prey on other seals or penguins. Leopard seals also feed on seabirds, fish, squid, and krill when their main food source is scarce. In water, the leopard seal is a powerful swimmer, but on land it cannot move quickly and does not therefore pose as much of a threat to other animals.

2 Seals close their nostrils when they swim underwater. This keeps air inside their lungs but water out. They can pursue their prey underwater for more than 30 minutes.

1 The body of the leopard seal is built for fast swimming. Its front flippers are long, helping it to swim and maneuver quickly.

3 The leopard seal has whiskers around its mouth and nose that detect movement in the water. This enables the seal to locate its prey when light conditions are poor.

Chinstrap penguin

6 The leopard seal swallows small penguins whole. It shakes larger penguins until their skin splits and then tears away portions of flesh.

4 The leopard seal's teeth are small but very sharp. The teeth are arranged like a sieve, and the seal can strain water through them. In this way, it can capture krill.

5 The mouth of the leopard seal is larger than the mouth of any other seal. This makes it easy to seize and swallow large prey.

Tigers

The tiger is found in Asia and lives in forests where there is plenty of cover. It hunts by creeping up on its prey and then ambushing it. Often, the prey can run faster than the tiger, and so it is very important that the tiger isn't spotted until the last moment. The tiger is a solitary hunter and prefers to feed on deer, wild pigs, and sometimes rhinoceros and elephant calves. It creeps straight toward its prey, crouching close to the ground so that it displays as little of itself as possible. When it is close enough, it makes a sudden leap and lands on the prey, knocking it over and pinning it down with its great weight.

2 The striped markings help to break up the tiger's outline, making it hard to see when it is hidden in the vegetation.

1 The long back legs have strong muscles in them to help the tiger spring forward at the last moment and catch the prey before it can escape.

3 In dense vegetation, the tiger often cannot see its prey. Acute hearing enables it to detect the slightest sound that its prey makes.

4 The tiger's large teeth and powerful jaws give the prey no chance of escaping. The back teeth are strong enough to crush bones.

Chital

5 The tiger has huge forepaws with five long, sharp claws. The claws rip into the prey and hold it securely as the tiger drags it to the ground.

6 The tiger usually eats mammals, such as the chital. Once it has caught its prey, it bites the animal on the back of the neck or the throat to kill it.

Glossary

Ampullae of Lorenzini
Sensory organs that cover the head and snout of sharks. They detect weak electrical fields emitted by other animals.

Beak
The name given to the visible mouthparts of animals such as birds and octopuses. They tear flesh from prey.

Camouflage
The coloring or markings of an animal that help to hide it in its surroundings

Carnivore
An animal that mainly, or only, eats meat

Compound eye
A large eye made up of many lenses. Each lens produces part of the complete image.

Constrictor
A snake that kills its prey by coiling around it and squeezing until the prey can no longer breathe

Drag
Resistance to movement through water

Echolocation
A method of finding food by using sound. It is used by animals such as fish-eating bats.

Facial disk
Special feathers on the face of the owl that help to pass sounds to its ears

Fangs
Long, sharp teeth, such as the two largest teeth of a snake, and the mouthparts of a spider. Poison travels through them into the prey.

Flipper
The limb of a seal that is shaped like a paddle for swimming

Herbivore
An animal that feeds on plants

Insect
An animal that has a body divided into three parts. It has six legs and sometimes one or two pairs of wings.

Jaws
Bones in the mouth that hold the teeth

Krill
Small sea animals that are related to shrimp. They are eaten by animals, such as leopard seals.

Ligament
Tissue that connects bones. In a snake, ligaments connecting the jawbones are very elastic and can stretch to allow the mouth to open wide.

Mammal
A warm-blooded animal that breathes air. Its young are born alive, and it feeds them on milk. Its body is usually covered with hair.

Mollusk
A soft-bodied animal without a skeleton. It usually lives inside a shell.

Paralyze
To prevent something from moving, often by injecting a poison

Placoid scales
Tiny toothlike projections that cover the skin of the shark. They protect the shark and help to reduce drag.

Predator
An animal that attacks and kills other animals for its food

Prey
An animal that is attacked and eaten by other animals

Radula
The tongue of a mollusk. It is kept inside the shell unless the mollusk is feeding or attacking its prey.

Reflex
An automatic movement made by an animal. Sometimes it is made to catch prey, or it can be an escape reaction.

Reptile
A cold-blooded animal with dry, scaly skin. Reptiles lay eggs on land.

Scales
Small, thin plates of hard skin that cover part of the body of an animal

Senses
These are sight, taste, hearing, smell, and touch. An animal uses them to obtain information about the outside world.

Siphon
A tube through which water enters or leaves the body of an animal, such as an octopus

Solitary
Living or hunting alone

Species
A group of animals that are of the same kind. They look alike and behave in similar ways. They are able to breed with each other but not usually with other species.

Spider
An animal with eight legs. It can produce silk and often spins webs to trap its prey.

Streamlined
A body which is smooth, sleek, and torpedo-shaped for easy movement through air or water

Sucker
A cup-shaped organ on the tentacle of an octopus that grips onto objects through suction

Talons
The sharp, hooked claws of birds, such as owls. Talons are strong enough to seize and kill prey.

Tentacle
A long, thin limb of animals, such as octopuses. A tentacle has no bones and can move in any direction.

True ears
Openings in the skull of the owl, one on each side, through which it hears. Feathers cover the openings.

Venom
A poison produced by animals such as snakes and spiders. It can paralyze or kill.

Vibration
A sound wave caused by an object moving quickly. Spiders can tell when their prey is nearby because of the vibrations it makes.

▶ Index